Günter Gerngross • Herbert Puchta

W0193148

Illustrations by Svjetlan Junaković

Layout by Gio Festin

PUBLISHED BY THE PRESS SYNDICATE OF THE UNIVERSITY OF CAMBRIDGE
The Pitt Building, Trumpington Street, Cambridge, United Kingdom
in association with Helbling, Rum/Innsbruck

CAMBRIDGE UNIVERSITY PRESS
The Edinburgh Building, Cambridge, CB2 2RU, UK www.cambridge.org
40 West 20th Street, New York, NY 10011-4211, USA
477 Williamstown Road, Port Melbourne, VIC 3207, Australia
Ruiz de Alarcón 13, 28014 Madrid, Spain
Dock House, The Waterfront, Cape Town 8001, South Africa

First published 1999
Seventh printing 2004

Printed in Austria

ISBN 0 521 65679 6 Activity Book
0 521 65683 4 Pupil's Book
0 521 65682 6 Teacher's Guide
0 521 65681 8 Picture Cards
0 521 65680 X Story Cards
0 521 65678 8 Class Audio Cassette
0 521 65677 X Class Audio CD
0 521 65676 1 Stories Video PAL
0 521 65675 3 Stories Video NTSC
0 521 65674 5 Stories Audio Cassette
0 521 65491 2 Stories Audio CD
0 521 65495 5 Activity Book Audio Cassette
0 521 65494 7 Activity Book Audio CD

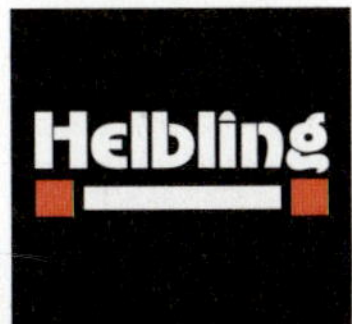

MARIA

ANDY

TOM

SANDRA

KAREN

BOB

MAX

BENNY

1, 2, 3,

5

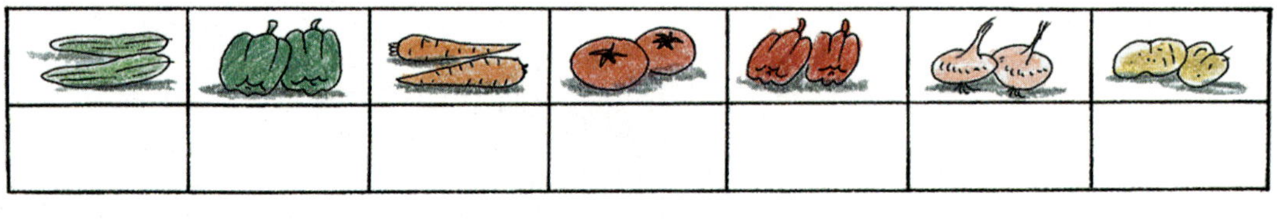

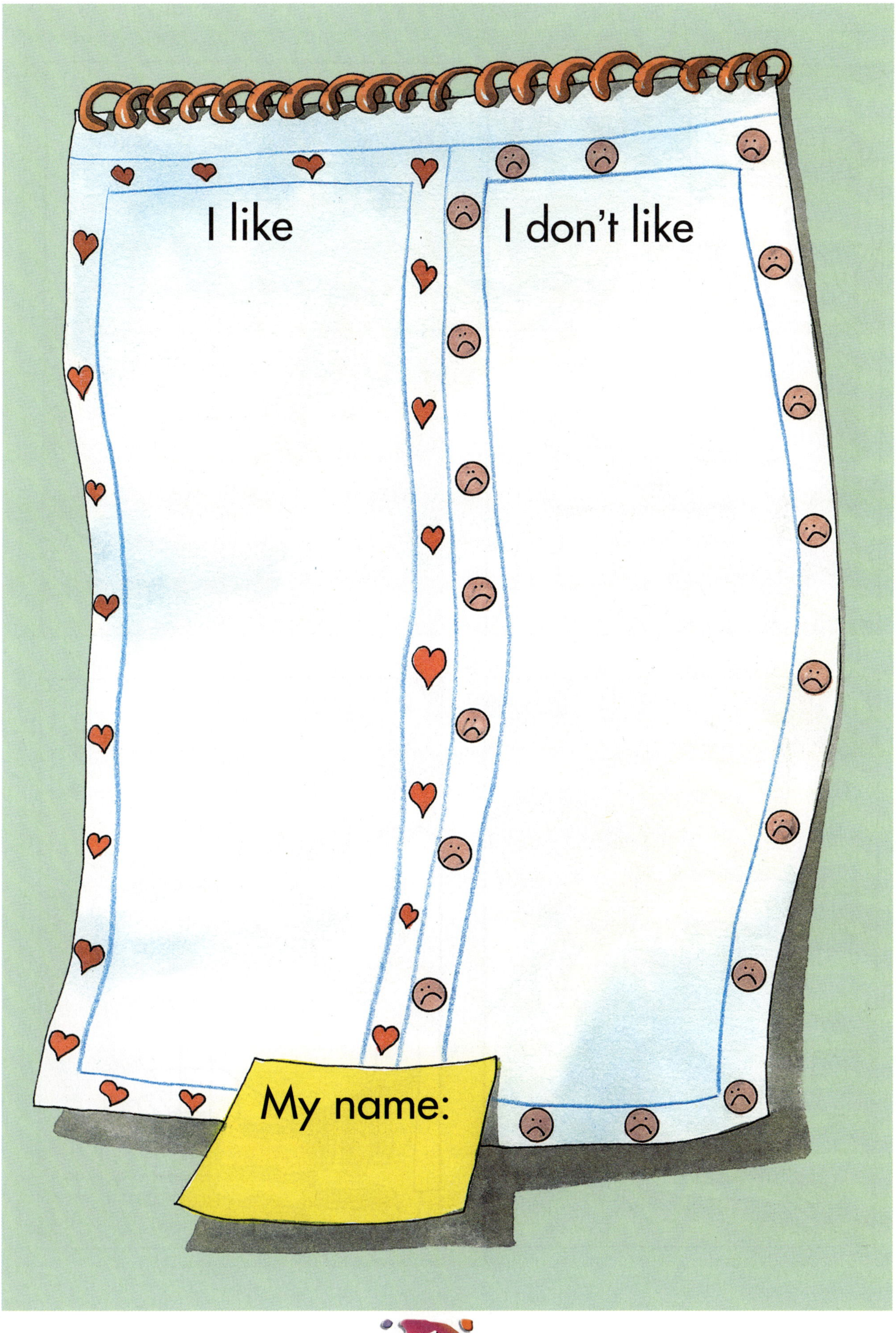

I like

I don't like

My name:

1

2

3

4

blue

red

yellow

green

pink

grey

orange

brown

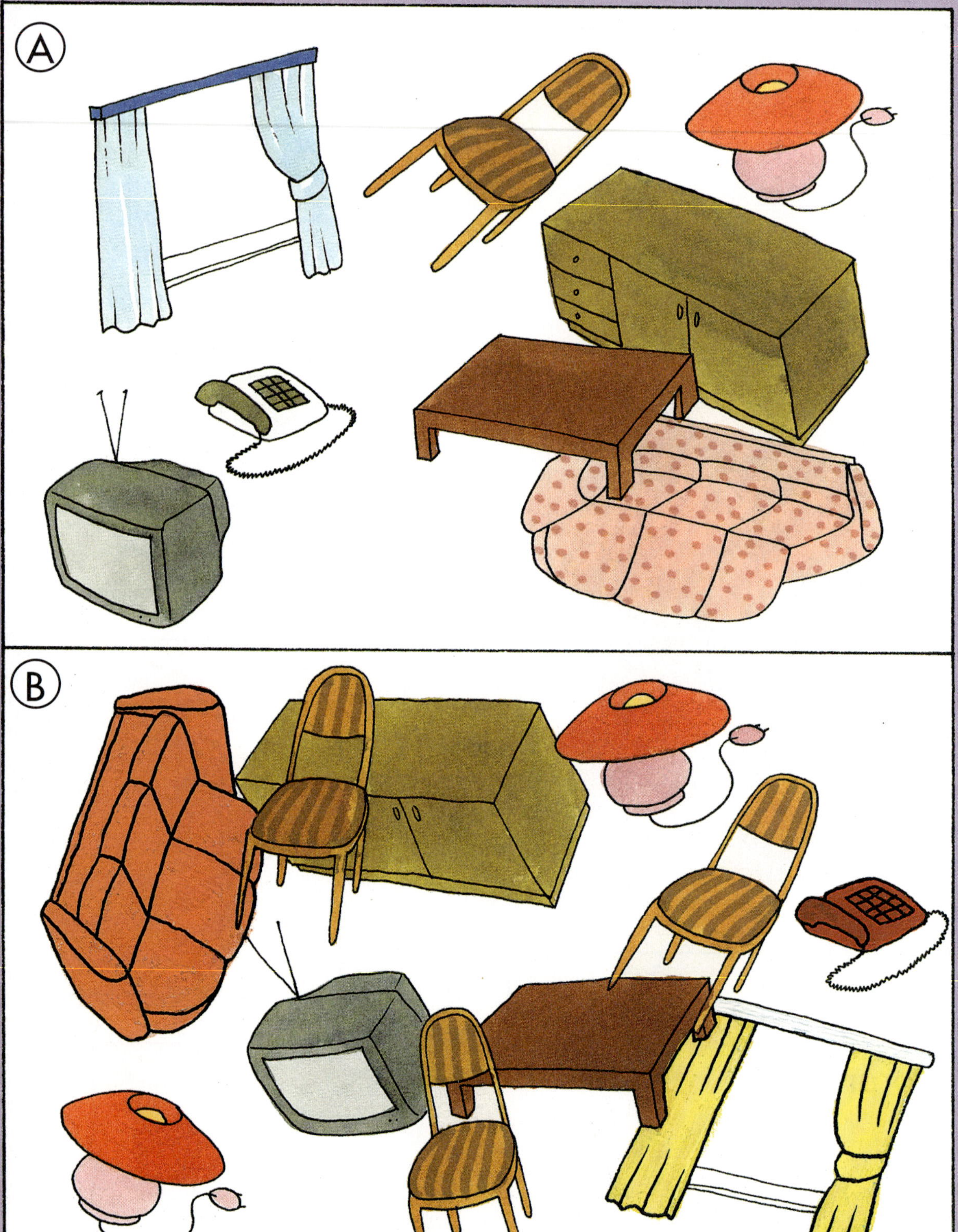

Ⓐ

Ⓑ

A

B

$4 + 5 + 1 = \square$

$3 + 2 + 4 = \square$

$10 - 6 + 1 = \square$

$7 - 4 + 5 = \square$

$9 - 3 - 4 = \square$

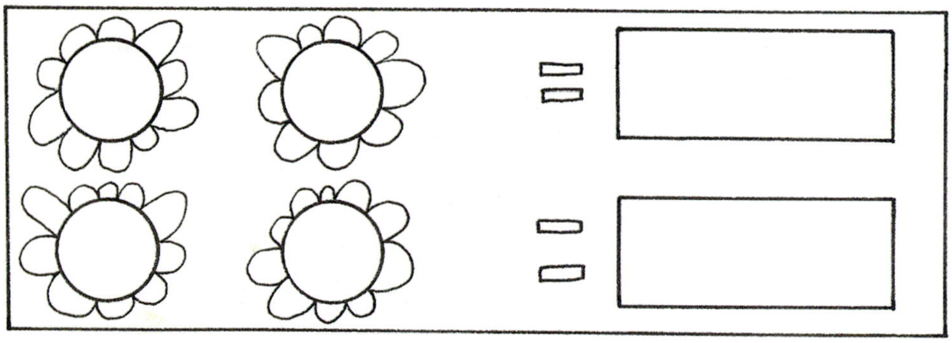

$\bigcirc \quad \bigcirc = \square$

$\bigcirc \quad \bigcirc = \square$

1

1

Linda

Benny

Mum

Dad

Grandpa

Grandma

Max

Where's my......?

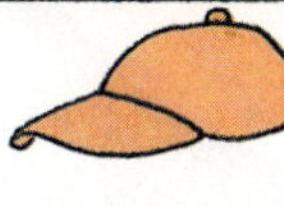

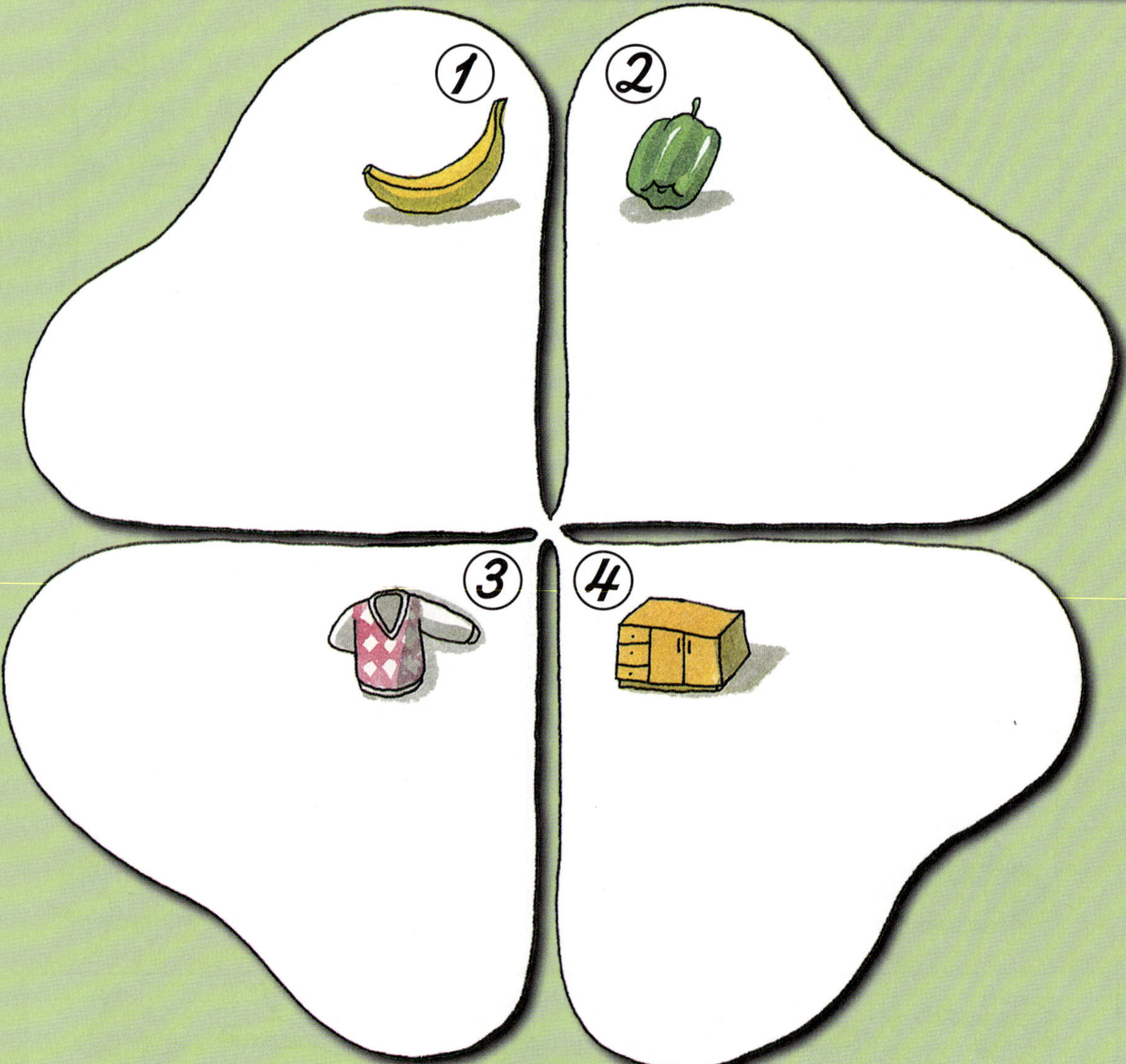

1

2

3

4

BINGO!

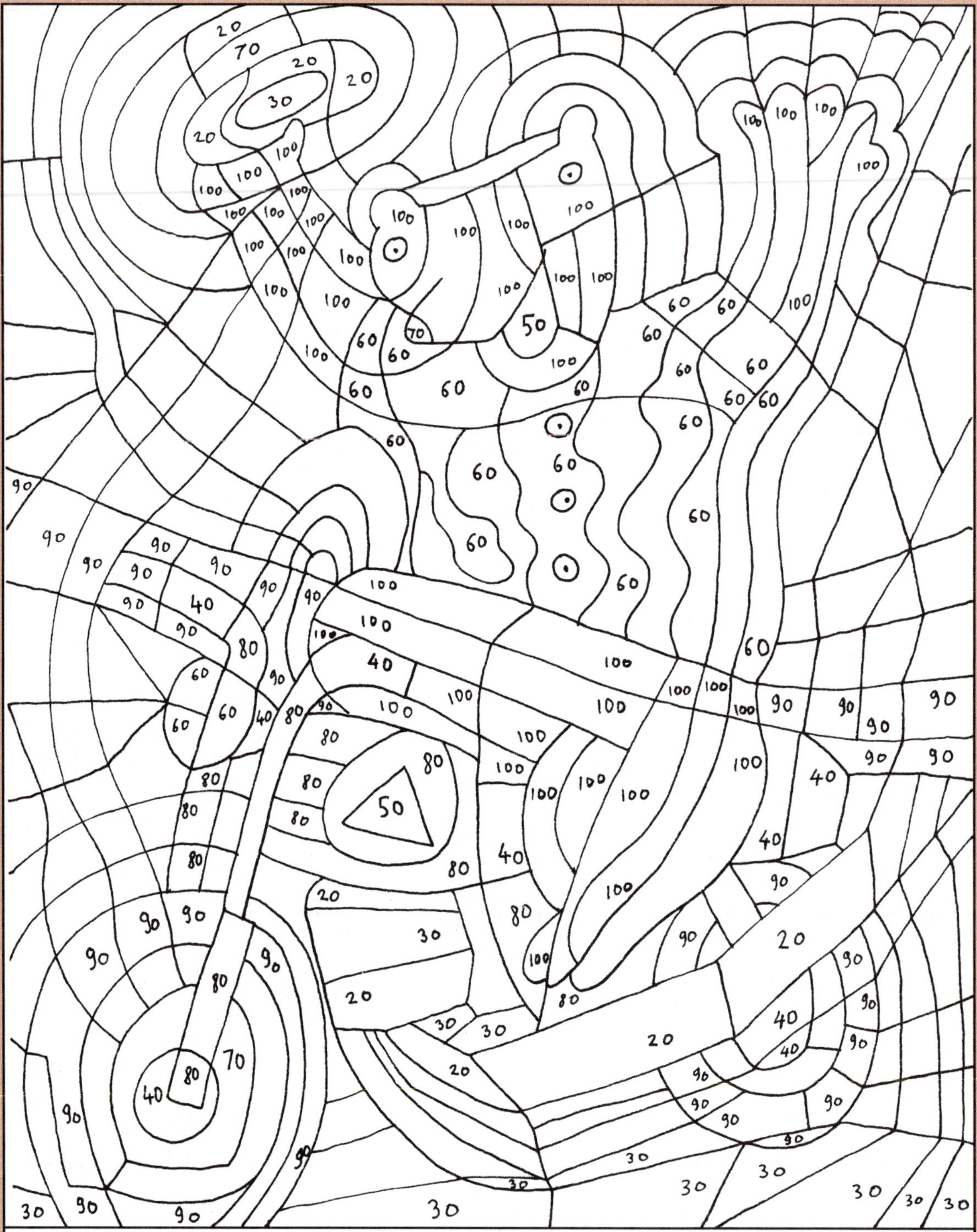

100 ☐ 90 ☐ 80 ☐ 70 ☐

60 ☐ 50 ☐ 40 ☐ 30 ☐ 20 ☐

100 20 70

0 40 60

90 10 80

50 30

fifty	twenty	thirty
seventy	ten	a hundred
eighty	zero	
sixty	forty	ninety

eyes

nose

hair

face

ears

arms

hands

legs

feet

Who is it?

5

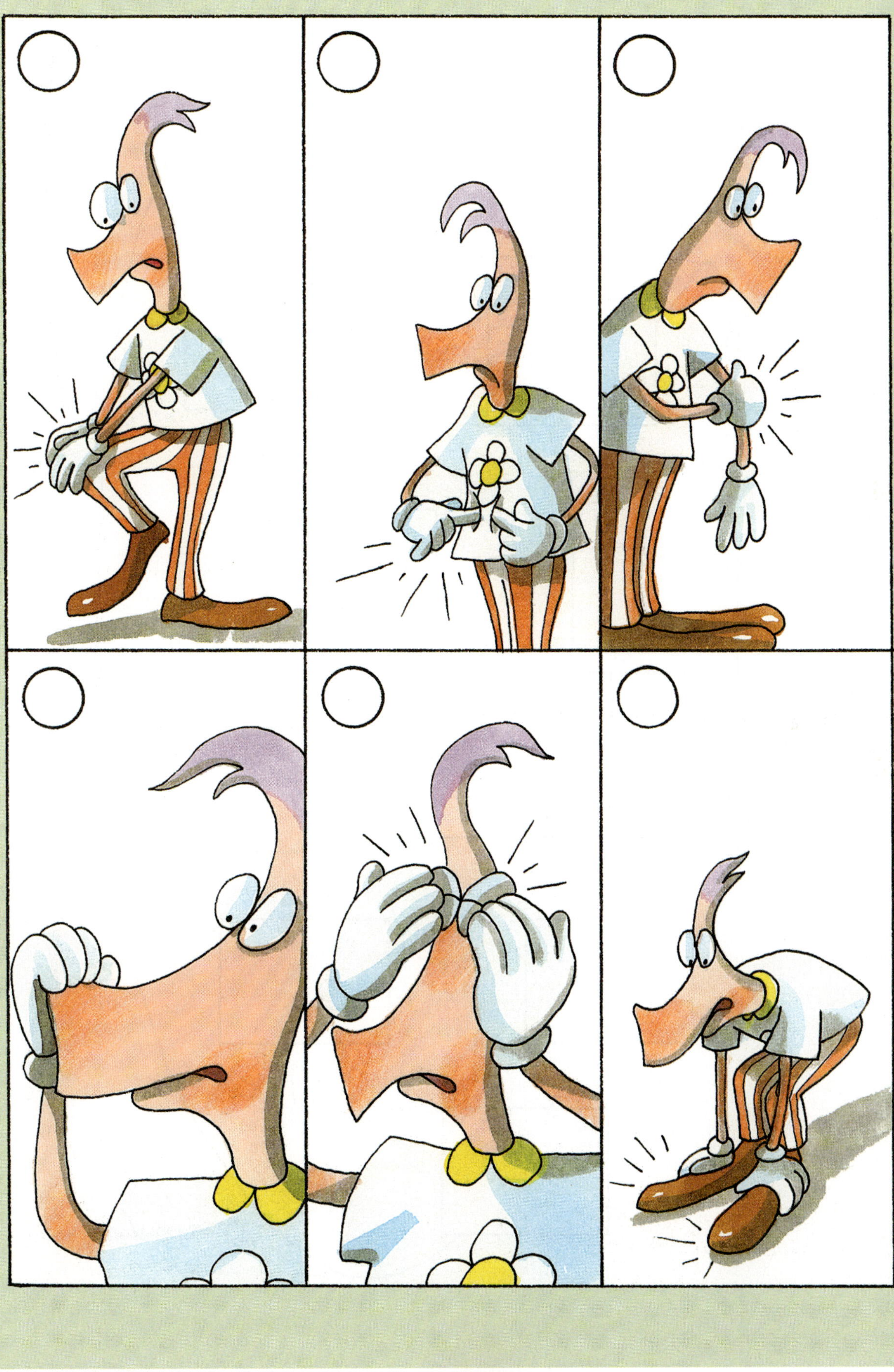

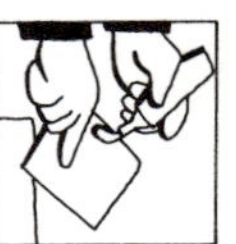
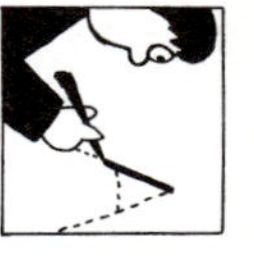

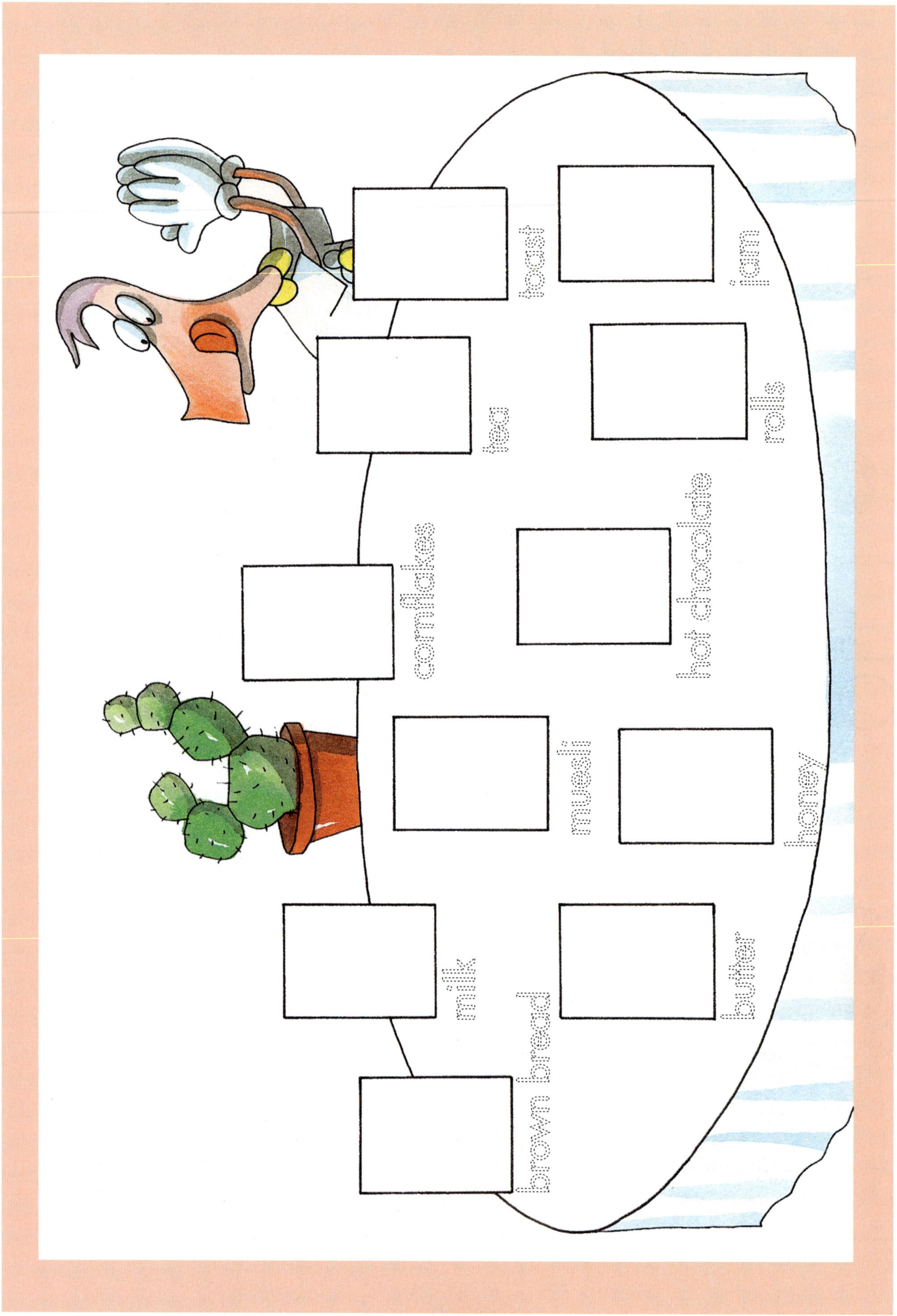

brown bread

milk

muesli

cornflakes

tea

toast

butter

honey

hot chocolate

rolls

jam

What do you like for breakfast?

M

T

W

Th

F

Sa

Su

plane

train

bus

underground

car

motorbike

bike

A

B

A

B

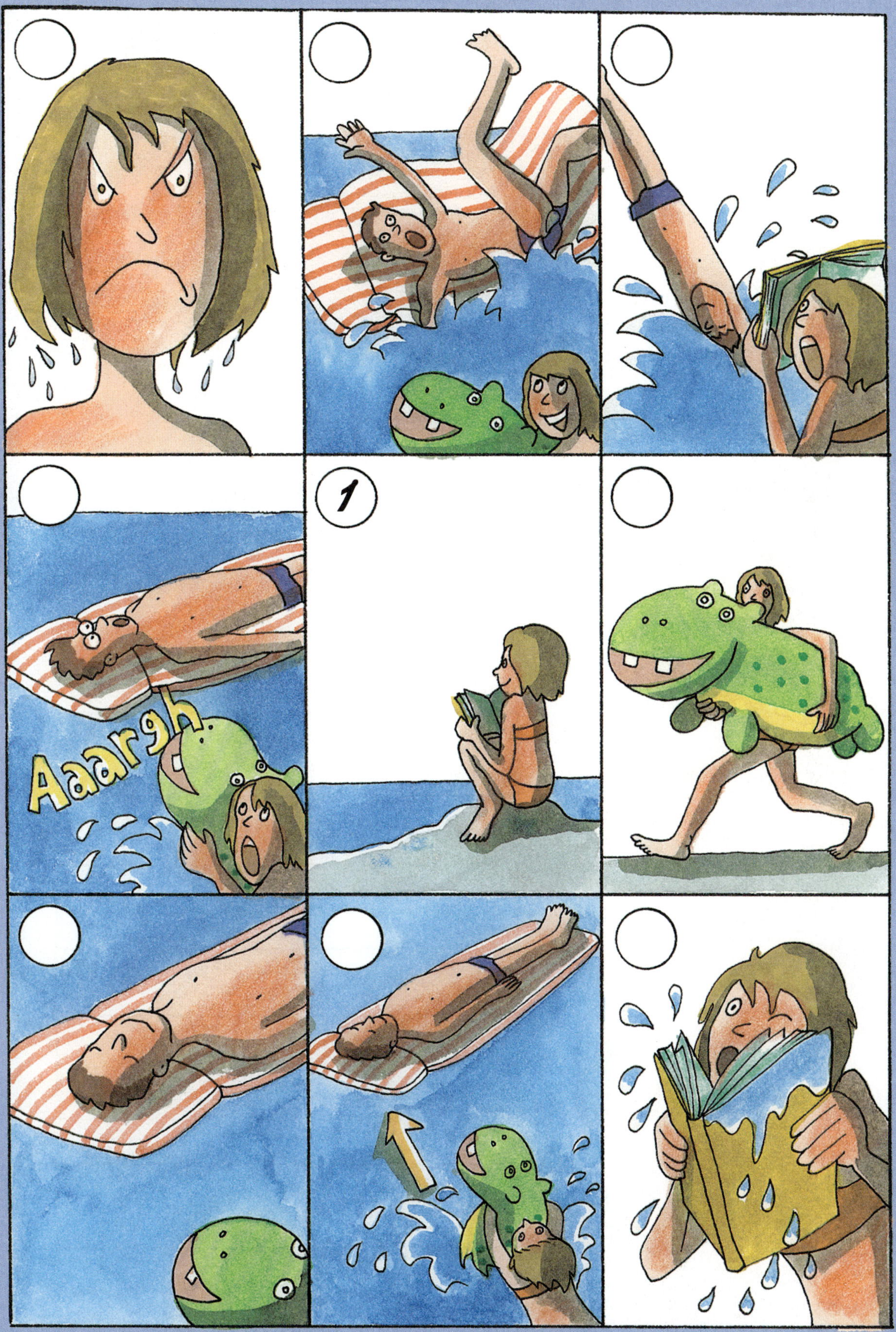

1

Aaargh

Blow a bubble.

Blow, blow.

Make it big.

Let it grow.

Linda

Ronnie

the sheep

Benny

Eddie

the mouse

Joe

the magician

the grasshopper

the frog

Max

Father Christmas

Fred

Maisie

Rosie

I like ________ best.

My number 2 is ______________ .

1	1	1	1
2	2	2	2
3	3	3	3
4	4	4	4

1	2	3	4	5
6	7	8	9	10

one	two	three	four
five	six	seven	eight
nine	ten		

black trainers	a green hat	a grey coat
a blue sweater	brown shoes	a yellow dress
orange socks	a red skirt	a pink cap

Mike | Debra | Susan | Frank

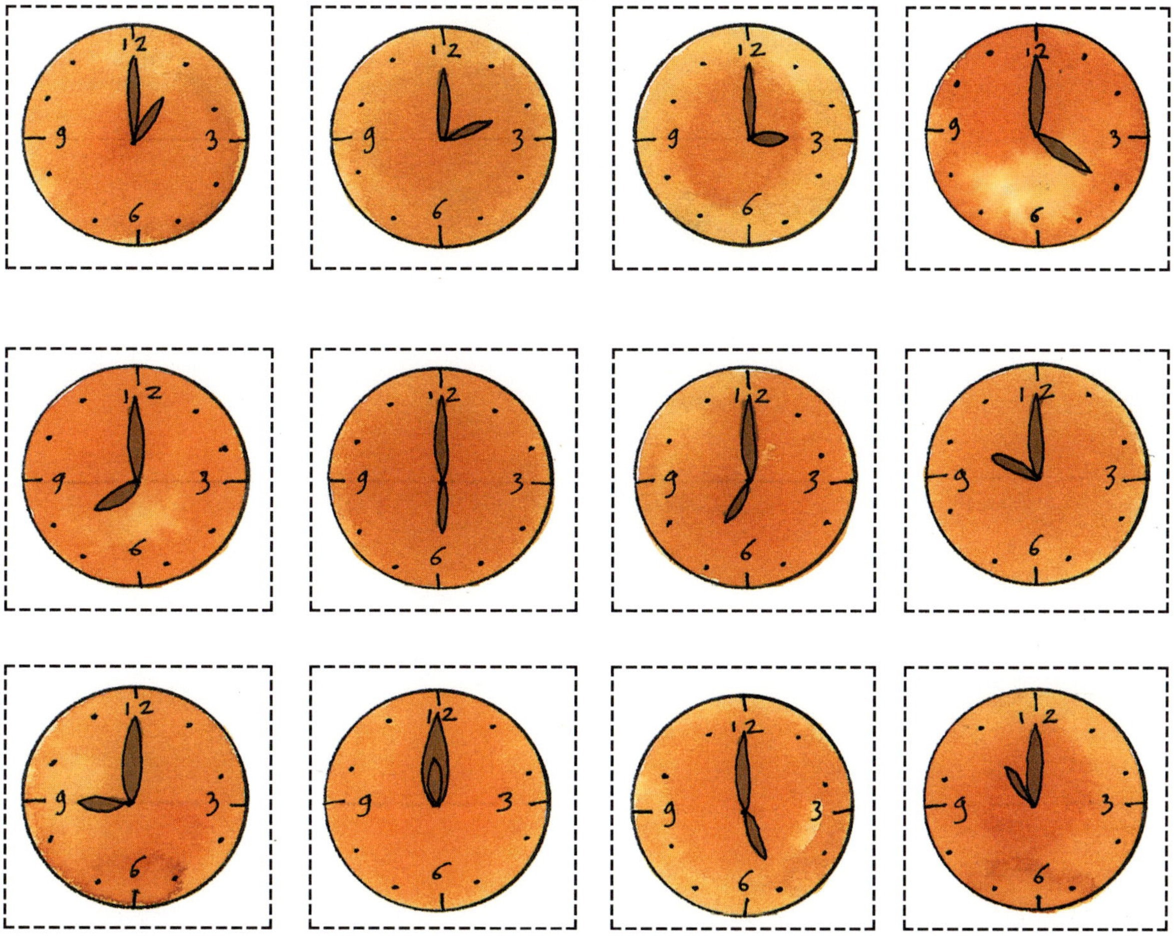

Biff

Boff

Taffy

Tiffy

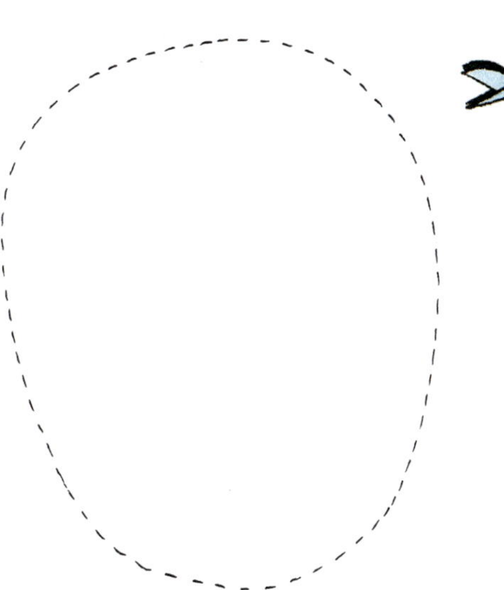

MUESLI

C

MUESLI

Then you fly

Hold on tight.

Through the sky.

Ahhh, the wind!